THE
LITTLE BOOK OF
SELF-CARE
FOR
CAPRICORN

Simple Ways to Refresh and Restore—According to the Stars

CONSTANCE STELLAS

ADAMS MEDIA
NEW YORK LONDON TORONTO SYDNEY NEW DELHI

Adams Media
An Imprint of Simon & Schuster, Inc.
57 Littlefield Street
Avon, Massachusetts 02322

First Adams Media hardcover edition January 2019

ADAMS MEDIA and colophon are trademarks of Simon & Schuster.

For information about special discounts for bulk purchases,
please contact Simon & Schuster Special Sales at 1-866-506-1949 or
business@simonandschuster.com.

The Simon & Schuster Speakers Bureau can bring authors to your live event. For
more information or to book an event contact the Simon & Schuster Speakers
Bureau at 1-866-248-3049 or visit our website at www.simonspeakers.com.

Interior design by Colleen Cunningham
Interior images © Getty Images; Clipart.com

Manufactured in the United States of America

10 9 8 7 6 5 4 3 2 1

Library of Congress Cataloging-in-Publication Data has been applied for.

ISBN 978-1-5072-0982-0
ISBN 978-1-5072-0983-7 (ebook)

Dedication

To my hardworking, funny Capricorn sister,
Libbie, with love.

CONTENTS

Acknowledgments

I would like to thank Karen Cooper and everyone at Adams Media who helped with this book. To Brendan O'Neill, Katie Corcoran Lytle, Sarah Doughty, Eileen Mullan, Casey Ebert, Sylvia Davis, and everyone else who worked on the manuscripts. To Frank Rivera, Colleen Cunningham, and Katrina Machado for their work on the book's cover and interior design. I appreciated your team spirit and eagerness to dive into the riches of astrology.

Introduction

It's time for you to have a little *"me" time*—powered by the zodiac. By tapping into your Sun sign's astrological and elemental energies, *The Little Book of Self-Care for Capricorn* brings star-powered strength and cosmic relief to your life with self-care guidance tailored specifically for you.

While you may enjoy steadily working toward your next challenge, Capricorn, this book focuses on your true self. This book provides information on how to incorporate self-care into your life while teaching you just how important astrology is to your overall self-care routine. You'll learn more about yourself as you learn about your sign and its governing element, earth. Then you can relax, rejuvenate, and stay balanced with more than one hundred self-care ideas and activities perfect for your Capricorn personality.

From meditations to ease worry to learning how to rock climb, you will find plenty of ways to heal your mind, body, and active spirit. Now, let the stars be your self-care guide!

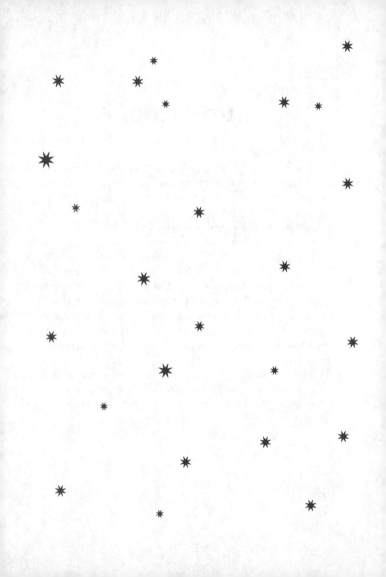

♑

PART 1

SIGNS, ELEMENTS, —— AND —— SELF-CARE

CHAPTER 1
WHAT IS SELF-CARE?

✳

Astrology gives insights into whom to love, when to charge forward into new beginnings, and how to succeed in whatever you put your mind to. When paired with self-care, astrology can also help you relax and reclaim that part of yourself that tends to get lost in the bustle of the day. In this chapter you'll learn what self-care is—for you. (No matter your sign, self-care is more than just lit candles and quiet reflection, though these activities may certainly help you find the renewal that you seek.) You'll also learn how making a priority of personalized self-care activities can benefit you in ways you may not even have thought of. Whether you're a Capricorn, a Pisces, or a Taurus, you deserve rejuvenation and renewal that's customized to your sign—this chapter reveals where to begin.

What Self-Care Is

Self-care is any activity that you do to take care of yourself. It rejuvenates your body, refreshes your mind, or realigns your spirit. It relaxes and refuels you. It gets you ready for a new day or a fresh start. It's the practices, rituals, and meaningful activities that you do, just for you, that help you feel safe, grounded, happy, and fulfilled.

The activities that qualify as self-care are amazingly unique and personalized to who you are, what you like, and, in large part, what your astrological sign is. If you're asking questions about what self-care practices are best for those ruled by earth and born under the determined eye of Capricorn, you'll find answers—and restoration—in Part 2. But, no matter which of those self-care activities speak to you and your unique place in the universe on any given day, it will fall into one of the following self-care categories—each of which pertains to a different aspect of your life:

* Physical self-care
* Emotional self-care
* Social self-care
* Mental self-care
* Spiritual self-care
* Practical self-care

When you practice all of these unique types of self-care—and prioritize your practice to ensure you are choosing the best options for your unique sign and governing element—know that you are actively working to create the version of yourself that the universe intends you to be.

Physical Self-Care

When you practice physical self-care, you make the decision to look after and restore the one physical body that has been bestowed upon you. Care for it. Use it in the best way you can imagine, for that is what the universe wishes you to do. You can't light the world on fire or move mountains if you're not doing everything you can to take care of your physical health.

Emotional Self-Care

Emotional self-care is when you take the time to acknowledge and care for your inner self, your emotional well-being. Whether you're angry or frustrated, happy or joyful, or somewhere in between, emotional self-care happens when you choose to sit with your emotions: when you step away from the noise of daily life that often drowns out or tamps down your authentic self. Emotional self-care lets you see your inner you as the cosmos intend. Once you identify your true emotions, you can either accept them and continue to move forward on your journey or you can try to change any negative emotions for the better. The more you acknowledge your feelings and practice emotional self-care, the more you'll feel the positivity that the universe and your life holds for you.

Social Self-Care

You practice social self-care when you nurture your relationships with others, be they friends, coworkers, or family members. In today's hectic world it's easy to let relationships fall to the wayside, but it's so important to share your life with others—and let others share their lives with you. Social self-care is reciprocal and often karmic. The support and love that you put out into the universe through social self-care is given back to you by those you socialize with—often tenfold.

Mental Self-Care

Mental self-care is anything that keeps your mind working quickly and critically. It helps you cut through the fog of the day, week, or year and ensures that your quick wit and sharp mind are intact and working the way the cosmos intended. Making sure your mind is fit helps you problem-solve, decreases stress since you're not feeling overwhelmed, and keeps you feeling on top of your mental game—no matter your sign or your situation.

Spiritual Self-Care

Spiritual self-care is self-care that allows you to tap into your soul and the soul of the universe and uncover its secrets. Rather than focusing on a particular religion or set of religious beliefs, these types of self-care activities reconnect you with a higher power: the sense that something out there is bigger than you. When you meditate, you connect. When you pray, you connect. Whenever you do something that allows you to experience and marry yourself to the vastness that is the cosmos, you practice spiritual self-care.

Practical Self-Care

Self-care is what you do to take care of yourself, and practical self-care, while not as expansive as the other types, is made up of the seemingly small day-to-day tasks that bring you peace and accomplishment. These practical self-care rituals are important, but are often overlooked. Scheduling a doctor's appointment that you've been putting off is practical self-care. Getting your hair cut is practical self-care. Anything you can check off your list of things to be accomplished gives you a sacred space to breathe and allows the universe more room to bring a beautiful sense of cosmic fulfillment your way.

What Self-Care Isn't

Self-care is restorative. Self-care is clarifying. Self-care is whatever you need to do to make yourself feel secure in the universe.

Now that you know what self-care is, it's also important that you're able to see what self-care isn't. Self-care is not something that you force yourself to do because you think it will be good for you. Some signs are energy in motion and sitting still goes against their place in the universe. Those signs won't feel refreshed by lying in a hammock or sitting down to meditate. Other signs aren't able to ground themselves unless they've found a self-care practice that protects their cosmic need for peace and quiet. Those signs won't find parties, concerts, and loud venues soothing or satisfying. If a certain ritual doesn't bring you peace, clarity, or satisfaction, then it's not right for your sign and you should find something that speaks to you more clearly.

There's a difference though between not finding satisfaction in a ritual that you've tried and not wanting to try a self-care activity because you're tired or stuck in a comfort zone. Sometimes going to the gym or meeting up with friends is the self-care practice that you need to experience—whether engaging in it feels like a downer or not. So consider how you feel when you're actually doing the activity. If it feels invigorating to get on the treadmill or you feel delight when you actually catch up with your friend, the ritual is doing what it should be doing and clearing space for you—among other benefits...

The Benefits of Self-Care

The benefits of self-care are boundless and there's none that's superior to helping you put rituals in place to feel more at home in your body, in your spirit, and in your unique home in the cosmos. There are, however, other benefits to engaging in the practice of self-care that you should know.

Rejuvenates Your Immune System

No matter which rituals are designated for you by the stars, your sign, and its governing element, self-care helps both your body and mind rest, relax, and recuperate. The practice of self-care activates the parasympathetic nervous system (often called the rest and digest system), which slows your heart rate, calms the body, and overall helps your body relax and release tension. This act of decompression gives your body the space it needs to build up and strengthen your immune system, which protects you from illness.

Helps You Reconnect—with Yourself

When you practice the ritual of self-care—especially when you customize this practice based on your personal sign and governing element—you learn what you like to do and what you need to do to replenish yourself. Knowing yourself better, and allowing yourself the time and space that you need to focus on your personal needs and desires, gives you the gifts of self-confidence and self-knowledge. Setting time aside to focus on your needs also helps you put busy, must-do things aside, which gives you time to reconnect with yourself and who you are deep inside.

Increases Compassion

Perhaps one of the most important benefits of creating a self-care ritual is that, by focusing on yourself, you become more compassionate to others as well. When you truly take the time to care for yourself and make yourself and your importance in the universe a priority in your own life, you're then able to care for others and see their needs and desires in a new way. You can't pour from an empty dipper, and self-care allows you the space and clarity to do what you can to send compassion out into the world.

Starting a Self-Care Routine

Self-care should be treated as a ritual in your life, something you make the time to pause for, no matter what. You are important. You deserve rejuvenation and a sense of relaxation. You need to open your soul to the gifts that the universe is giving you, and self-care provides you with a way to ensure you're ready to receive those gifts. To begin a self-care routine, start by making yourself the priority. Do the customized rituals in Part 2 with intention, knowing the universe has already given them to you, by virtue of your sign and your governing element.

Now that you understand the role that self-care will hold in your life, let's take a closer look at the connection between self-care and astrology.

CHAPTER 2

SELF-CARE AND ASTROLOGY

✳

Astrology is the study of the connection between the objects in the heavens (the planets, the stars) and what happens here on earth. Just as the movements of the planets and other heavenly bodies influence the ebb and flow of the tides, so do they influence you—your body, your mind, your spirit. This relationship is ever present and is never more important—or personal—than when viewed through the lens of self-care.

In this chapter you'll learn how the locations of these celestial bodies at the time of your birth affect you and define the self-care activities that will speak directly to you as an Aries, a Leo, a Capricorn, or any of the other zodiac signs. You'll see how the zodiac influences every part of your being and why ignoring its lessons can leave you feeling frustrated and unfulfilled. You'll also realize that, when you perform the rituals of self-care based on your sign, the wisdom of the cosmos will lead you down a path of fulfillment and restoration—to the return of who you really are, deep inside.

Zodiac Polarities

In astrology, all signs are mirrored by other signs that are on the opposite side of the zodiac. This polarity ensures that the zodiac is balanced and continues to flow with an unbreakable, even stream of energy. There are two different polarities in the zodiac and each is called by a number of different names:

* Yang/masculine/positive polarity
* Yin/feminine/negative polarity

Each polar opposite embodies a number of opposing traits, qualities, and attributes that will influence which self-care practices will work for or against your sign and your own personal sense of cosmic balance.

Yang
Whether male or female, those who fall under yang, or masculine, signs are extroverted and radiate their energy outward. They are spontaneous, active, bold, and fearless. They move forward in life with the desire to enjoy everything the

world has to offer to them, and they work hard to transfer their inspiration and positivity to others so that those individuals may experience the same gifts that the universe offers them. All signs governed by the fire and air elements are yang and hold the potential for these dominant qualities. We will refer to them with masculine pronouns. These signs are:

* Aries
* Leo
* Sagittarius
* Gemini
* Libra
* Aquarius

There are people who hold yang energy who are introverted and retiring. However, by practicing self-care that is customized for your sign and understanding the potential ways to use your energy, you can find a way—perhaps one that's unique to you—to claim your native buoyancy and dominance and engage with the path that the universe opens for you.

Yin

Whether male or female, those who fall under yin, or feminine, signs are introverted and radiate inwardly. They draw people and experiences to them rather than seeking people and experiences in an extroverted way. They move forward in life with an energy that is reflective, receptive, and focused on communication and achieving shared goals. All signs governed by the earth and water elements are yin and hold the potential for these reflective qualities. We will refer to them with feminine pronouns. These signs are:

* Taurus
* Virgo
* Capricorn
* Cancer
* Scorpio
* Pisces

As there are people with yang energy who are introverted and retiring, there are also people with yin energy who are outgoing and extroverted. And by practicing self-care rituals that speak to your particular sign, energy, and governing body, you will reveal your true self and the balance of energy will be maintained.

Governing Elements

Each astrological sign has a governing element that defines their energy orientation and influences both the way the sign moves through the universe and relates to self-care. The elements are fire, earth, air, and water. All these signs in each element share certain characteristics, along with having their own sign-specific qualities:

* **Fire:** Fire signs are adventurous, bold, and energetic. They enjoy the heat and warm environments and look to the sun and fire as a means to recharge their depleted batteries. They're competitive, outgoing, and passionate. The fire signs are Aries, Leo, and Sagittarius.
* **Earth:** Earth signs all share a common love and tendency toward a practical, material, sensual, and economic orientation. The earth signs are Taurus, Virgo, and Capricorn.
* **Air:** Air is the most ephemeral element and those born under this element are thinkers, innovators, and communicators. The air signs are Gemini, Libra, and Aquarius.
* **Water:** Water signs are instinctual, compassionate, sensitive, and emotional. The water signs are Cancer, Scorpio, and Pisces.

Chapter 3 teaches you all about the ways your specific governing element influences and drives your connection to your cosmically chosen self-care rituals, but it's important that you realize how important these elemental traits are to your self-care practice and to the activities that will help restore and reveal your true self.

Sign Qualities

Each of the astrological elements governs three signs. Each of these three signs is also given its own quality or mode, which corresponds to a different part of each season: the beginning, the middle, or the end.

* **Cardinal signs:** The cardinal signs initiate and lead in each season. Like something that is just starting out, they are actionable, enterprising, and assertive, and are born leaders. The cardinal signs are Aries, Cancer, Libra, and Capricorn.
* **Fixed signs:** The fixed signs come into play when the season is well established. They are definite, consistent, reliable, motivated by principles, and powerfully stubborn. The fixed signs are Taurus, Leo, Scorpio, and Aquarius.
* **Mutable signs:** The mutable signs come to the forefront when the seasons are changing. They are part of one season, but also part of the next. They are adaptable, versatile, and flexible. The mutable signs are Gemini, Virgo, Sagittarius, and Pisces.

Each of these qualities tells you a lot about yourself and who you are. They also give you invaluable information about the types of self-care rituals that your sign will find the most intuitive and helpful.

Ruling Planets

In addition to qualities and elements, each specific sign is ruled by a particular planet that lends its personality to those born under that sign. Again, these sign-specific traits give you valuable insight into the personality of the signs and the self-care rituals that may best rejuvenate them. The signs that correspond to each planet—and the ways that those planetary influences determine your self-care options—are as follows:

* **Aries:** Ruled by Mars, Aries is passionate, energetic, and determined.
* **Taurus:** Ruled by Venus, Taurus is sensual, romantic, and fertile.
* **Gemini:** Ruled by Mercury, Gemini is intellectual, changeable, and talkative.
* **Cancer:** Ruled by the Moon, Cancer is nostalgic, emotional, and home loving.
* **Leo:** Ruled by the Sun, Leo is fiery, dramatic, and confident.
* **Virgo:** Ruled by Mercury, Virgo is intellectual, analytical, and responsive.
* **Libra:** Ruled by Venus, Libra is beautiful, romantic, and graceful.
* **Scorpio:** Ruled by Mars and Pluto, Scorpio is intense, powerful, and magnetic.
* **Sagittarius:** Ruled by Jupiter, Sagittarius is optimistic, boundless, and larger than life.

* **Capricorn:** Ruled by Saturn, Capricorn is wise, patient, and disciplined.
* **Aquarius:** Ruled by Uranus, Aquarius is independent, unique, and eccentric.
* **Pisces:** Ruled by Neptune and Jupiter, Pisces is dreamy, sympathetic, and idealistic.

A Word on Sun Signs

When someone is an Aries, Leo, Sagittarius, or any of the other zodiac signs, it means that the sun was positioned in this constellation in the heavens when they were born. Your Sun sign is a dominant factor in defining your personality, your best self-care practices, and your soul nature. Every person also has the position of the Moon, Mercury, Venus, Mars, Jupiter, Saturn, Uranus, Neptune, and Pluto. These planets can be in any of the elements: fire signs, earth signs, air signs, or water signs. If you have your entire chart calculated by an astrologer or on an Internet site, you can see the whole picture and learn about all your elements. Someone born under Leo with many signs in another element will not be as concentrated in the fire element as someone with five or six planets in Leo. Someone born in Pisces with many signs in another element will not be as concentrated in the water element as someone with five or six planets in Pisces. And so on. Astrology is a complex system and has many shades of meaning. For our purposes, looking at the self-care practices designated by your Sun sign, or what most people consider their sign, will give you the information you need to move forward and find fulfillment and restoration.

CHAPTER 3

ESSENTIAL ELEMENTS:
EARTH

✳

The earth element is most familiar to all of us, for the earth is our home. We are born on this planet and are the custodians of her beauty, natural resources, health, and well-being. There is an intimate connection between human beings and the balance of the earth's conditions. The earth signs (Taurus, Virgo, and Capricorn) feel this connection more than other signs, and their approach to self-care reflects their relationship with this natural element. They are practical and realistic, and they need self-care techniques that match their disposition. More so, earth signs are rooted in the material, physical world. They are, at their best, pragmatic, sensual, patient, and grounded. At their worst they can be greedy, lascivious, and materialistic.

Most humans face the polarity of balancing the need and competition of making a living, with the dreams and desires of their heart. Earth signs accept this as reality instead of fighting against it. Becoming successful in the material world is their natural inclination. Any self-care they do must reflect that ultimate goal as well. Let's take a look at the mythological importance of the earth and its counterparts, the basic characteristics of the three earth signs, and what they all have in common when it comes to self-care.

The Mythology of Earth

There are many creation myths from all over the world. Most of these myths feature a Mother Earth figure. In Greek mythology, which forms the basis for much of astrology, Gaia was the Earth Mother. She represented the circle of life. Gaia came out of chaos and gave birth to Ouranos, the sky god, who also happened to be her husband. (The Greeks liked to keep things in the family.) The relationship between Gaia and Ouranos was so passionate that their children could not emerge from Gaia's womb. One of these unborn children was Cronos who in Roman astrology was called Saturn. Cronos decided to overthrow Ouranos and in the womb emasculated his father. And the sky separated from the earth. Cronos, the lord of time, ruled the universe for a time but later got his comeuppance as Zeus/Jupiter displaced him and became the chief god and ruler of all. These myths regarding the separation of earth and sky (or heaven and earth) abound in ancient world cultures.

Earth signs strive for measured success, and often seek worldly possessions to solidify their self-worth. This need for stability is indicative of their element. Earth, after all, is the foundation for life. It is tangible, solid, and defined. Many earth signs are so grounded in reality they can lose track of their emotional well-being. Self-care rituals that cater to both mind and soul are key for earth signs. Simplicity and practicality are often paramount.

The Element of Earth

Earth signs are known for their measured approach to life. They are typically patient, reliable, and disciplined, traits that often lead to prosperity. Because of this, earth signs are often viewed as well balanced and levelheaded, hence the saying *down-to-earth*. Earth signs are known as the sensible, pragmatic signs, choosing to focus on practical solutions over emotions. They are not light and buoyant like air signs, passionate and fiery like fire signs, nor empathetic and fluid like water signs. Instead, they are committed, strong, and trustworthy. For example, Taurus is loyal and always ready to help friends and family in need. Virgo is hardworking and will never back down from a challenge. And Capricorn is responsible and will help others stick to their responsibilities as well.

Astrological Symbols

The astrological symbols (also called the zodiacal symbols) of the earth signs also give you hints as to how earth signs move through the world. Each symbol ties back to the nature associated with earth signs:

* Taurus is the Bull
* Virgo is the Maiden gathering the harvest
* Capricorn is the Goat

All these signs show steadfast and intimate harmony with the cycles of the seasons and a personal connection with the earth: the meadows, green fields, and rocks. Taurus comes from ancient myths about the cults that worshipped the bull as a fertility symbol. She represents coiled power not yet unleashed. Virgo is the only earth sign that has a human symbol. She is a mutable sign and like a junior Mother Earth. Capricorn is of the earth but climbs the mountains of ambition and spiritual ascent. Each earth sign's personality and subsequent approach to self-care connect to the qualities of these representative symbols.

Signs and Seasonal Modes

Each of the elements in astrology also has a sign that corresponds to a different part of each season.

* **Fixed:** Taurus, the first earth sign, comes when spring is in full bloom. Taurus is called a fixed earth sign because she comes when the season is well established. The fixed signs are definite, motivated by principles, and powerfully stubborn.
* **Mutable:** Virgo, the second earth sign, moves us from summer to autumn. These signs are called mutable. In terms of character the mutable signs are changeable and flexible.
* **Cardinal:** Capricorn is the leader of the earth signs because she marks the beginning of winter and the time around the winter solstice.

If you know your element and whether you are a cardinal, fixed, or mutable sign, you know a lot about yourself. This is invaluable for self-care and is reflected in the customized earth sign self-care rituals found in Part 2.

Earth Signs and Self-Care

The earth signs' first motivation in life is to feel comfortable in their physical surroundings. For physical self-care their most important motivation is routine and diligence. Earth signs don't require a lot of variety. Their motto is, "If something works, keep it." The downside to this attitude is that earth signs can get stuck in a rut, but the benefits of continuous physical exercise, self-care, and good diet at all ages are the cornerstones of comfort for earth signs.

You may notice that earth signs touch other people more frequently than other elements do. They pat, reach out, hug, and extend themselves physically to others. They also have an intimate and close sense of personal space and will be upfront and personal in encountering new people or old friends. They want and need to sense the whole person.

Earth signs take self-care actions in a very practical way. For example, if an earth sign wants to exercise more, they may think the following: "If I can exercise more, I will lose weight and be healthier, so I will have more years to build my business, enjoy my family, and do what I want."

Spiritually, earth signs feel little division between body and soul. If they feel comfortable and well physically, then their soul qualities can evolve and blossom. Some people may feel that the high-minded notion of spiritual retreat and meditation defines a spiritual person, and they therefore look down on an earth sign's practical thoughts, such as "How much will it cost to go on this retreat and how much time will it take?" Earth signs don't consider this to be materialism at the expense of spirituality. Instead, to them, it is a clear recognition of the practical and sensible way the world works. Ashrams, well-being programs, herbs, and health practices cost money, and it is a reasonable question to ask if the practice is worth it.

The most important "rule" for earth signs is that self-care feed the senses. Whatever the plan is, it should include every sense. The activity must look appealing, smell good, taste good, sound good, and feel good. The more all the senses are involved, the happier the earth signs will be and the more likely they will be to follow the program. If the price is reasonable, so much the better. But too much sensual input can cause earth signs to overindulge and become lethargic. This is a potential pitfall for all the earth signs.

The overall purpose and meaning of the earth signs is to offer practical solutions to maintain personal self-care and the health of the planet. The earth signs have a lot to teach the people around them. Modern life is increasingly jagged. The earth signs demonstrate the value of solid measured progress. Walk don't run, and take things as they come. This attitude can preserve each of us as well as planet earth.

So now that you know what earth signs need to practice self-care, let's look at each of the pragmatic characteristics of Capricorn and how she can maintain her inner balance.

CHAPTER 4

SELF-CARE FOR CAPRICORN

✳

Dates: December 22–January 19
Element: Earth
Polarity: Yin
Quality: Cardinal
Symbol: Goat
Ruler: Saturn

Capricorn is the last earth sign of the zodiac. She is a powerful cardinal sign, and her season begins around the winter solstice (the winter and summer solstices represent respectively the nadir of the sun with the shortest days and the height of sunlight with the longest days). Ancient peoples celebrated the winter solstice because it marked the pivot of the sun's motion from darkness to light.

Shortly after the winter solstice, the sun gains seconds, minutes, and then hours of light. Ancient sacred spaces such as the Karnak Temple, in Egypt; Stonehenge, in England; and Newgrange, in Ireland, were built to catch the solstice light as it beamed through specially designed architecture. The return of the sun was a religious and spiritual renewal that blessed all people. The winter solstice is still celebrated today in these sacred spaces.

The cardinal fire sign, Aries, begins the astrological year and the cardinal earth sign, Capricorn, ends the calendar year. Metaphorically, the leadership spark that Aries initiates can only be realized in the world through the practical and structural orientation of Capricorn. Slowly and steadily, Capricorn will build structures and get where she wants to go.

Saturn is Capricorn's ruling planet. In ancient times Saturn was the farthest planet that could be seen with the naked eye. In Roman mythology Saturn (Cronos in Greek mythology) was the lord of time. He also ruled challenges, delays, and old age. He was a powerful god, but not a cheery one. The Romans respected him for the power of his wisdom and patience. Indeed, in Roman mythology when Saturn fled from Mount Olympus to Italy, his rule there initiated a golden age and time when people lived in perfect harmony. The feast of Saturnalia was held every year during the winter. During this time, it was forbidden to declare war, slaves and masters ate at the same table, and people gave each other gifts. Saturnalia eventually developed into the Christian holiday of Christmas. Many contemporary holidays have their origins in the progression of the astronomical cycles (which forms the basis for the astrological signs). The winter solstice, or beginning of

Capricorn, marks the return of the light, and Christians believe that the birth of Christ brought light to the world.

The planet Saturn is called a malefic planet in astrology because its influence delays or hinders activity. People don't usually enjoy the effects of Saturn, because under his influence we are forced to think concretely, to plan, and to consider all the real-world ramifications of our actions. But we all need the reality check Saturn offers. If you are Capricorn, you have this quality naturally. You patiently, diligently, and steadily climb toward your goal.

Capricorn considers life serious business and is very interested in achieving success. Sometimes the success she achieves is in intangible, spiritual realms; sometimes success is purely material. The best of Capricorn's qualities blend practical realities with a sense of mission and high mindedness. The worst of Capricorn traits can be ruthlessness and obsession to achieve her ambitions at any cost. Capricorn's most significant trait is the fervor with which she approaches all her endeavors and causes. Capricorn's strong power instinct, drive, patience, and work ethic sustain her while she climbs toward her goals.

Self-Care and Capricorn

In terms of self-care and well-being, Capricorn is enigmatic. She realizes that she must be strong, fit, and healthy to achieve her goals, but launching self-care and being mindful of her own needs do not come naturally. She is devoted to action and self-improvement, but may need lessons in how to temper her drive with softness and kindness to herself.

The best approach for success is for Capricorn to realize that "things must get done." And in her case the things that must get done are taking care of her health and learning to relax and laugh. If Capricorn sees self-care as a mission she must accomplish, she will learn to implement and perhaps even enjoy self-care. It is merely a matter of applying her strong will to the necessary goal of self-care.

Once Capricorn realizes that self-care is useful to her, she is very pragmatic and successful. Capricorn rules structure and hierarchy and if ill, she has a talent for finding good care. She usually knows qualified medical people, and through diligence she will connect with professionals who can truly help her. For everyday care Capricorn tends to know where to find the best products for well-being and maintenance. She loves to share this knowledge with her acquaintances, family, and friends.

Capricorn Rules the Bones

Capricorn rules the skeletal structure, all the bones, the joints, the knees, and the teeth. Maintaining calcium and good nutrition is an essential habit for her. Frequently Capricorn has dental problems and should follow through on all checkups. In the skeletal system Capricorn's weak area is the knees. Heavy-impact sports are not the best for Capricorn. If Capricorn is a jogger, she needs to be vigilant about sneakers. They should specifically be for jogging and should be changed frequently. When possible she should jog on earth rather than concrete. If she uses a treadmill, she should alternate with the elliptical jogger, which is softer on the joints.

Capricorn is not casual about exercise and sports. She pursues her goals in the same determined fashion as with work, love, or money. Capricorn needs to be aware that it will be hard for her to back away from her goal even if it is causing pain and difficulty. Too much bodily stress will not be beneficial in the long run. If Capricorn tunes into her body, she will have the answer to whether to press on or stop. Developing this sense of "enough" is a crucial skill in self-care.

Capricorn and Self-Care Success

Capricorn can get so involved in her own work that self-care falls by the wayside. She pushes herself and then becomes exhausted. And, of course, all the good striving she has done must stop while she regains her balance and well-being. Why not prevent burnout before it occurs? Capricorn's disciplined approach and persistence can easily be adapted to taking care of herself. And then she will truly be of use to herself and to others.

A way to keep in healthy balance is to make room for laughing. It sounds silly to say make room for such a natural human reaction, but the problems and injustices of the world can gnaw at Capricorn's sense of responsibility, and she feels she must go out and rescue the situation. Laughing at the entire array of human weaknesses and strengths is the antidote to an overserious approach to life. There is a guru known as the laughing guru; he and his followers get together and have laughing sessions. This would be a great activity for Cap and would put her on the road to success in self-care and whatever else she wants to do.

Psychological counseling is of interest to Capricorn only in so far as it makes her more effective in her work life. She may consider therapy, unless in crisis, an indulgence. She is always interested in ways to improve her usefulness in the world and more efficient ways of getting to her goals, but a leisurely examination of childhood traumas or her home life only becomes important if her life is not functioning the way she would like it to. Capricorn is a leader and not particularly interested in the complexities of how someone else is feeling. She says, "Let's just get the job done." Capricorn avidly reads books about the habits of successful people, and this can form the basis of her inner therapy and sense of well-being.

The soul work for Capricorn usually involves lessons in the exercise of power with humility. Pride and domination are qualities that can hinder Capricorn's true power and leadership abilities. When she uses her strength to be of use to others, rather than using people and situations for her own expedience, Capricorn can be very evolved.

Capricorn is also very loyal to friends and family. Her loyalty extends to her principles and devotion to causes. Once she commits to a set of beliefs, she does not waver. If she has the means, she is extremely charitable but only after thoroughly researching the business structure and how the donated money is spent. Capricorn doesn't treat money or commitments lightly.

Capricorn shares a sense of duty and engagement that benefits us all. She feels responsible to do her best to improve the world. If we follow her lead, we can all reach the summit of whatever mountain we attempt to climb.

PART 2

SELF-CARE
RITUALS
— FOR —
CAPRICORN

Plan a Family Dinner

Capricorn feels strongly about the past and family traditions; reliable and stable, she often takes on the responsibility of being the glue that holds family (or friends or loved ones) together. So why not embrace that family-centered side of yourself and plan a family dinner for your loved ones?

Get everyone together to share in stories, memories, and fun times. As a Capricorn you will feel rewarded and comforted by the family togetherness, and it will also be a whole lot of fun! Remember, it doesn't have to be a fancy gathering (although you do love a sophisticated get-together). Any size and style of dinner will do. It's all about taking time and reconnecting with your family and loved ones, and letting them know how important they are to you.

Break Free from
Your Comfort Zone

As an earth sign, you tend to be organized, ritualistic, and highly structured. However, because you like structure and rituals so much, you can easily fall into repeating patterns, and even if that pattern is not particularly healthy, you'll stay with it. Once you're in a comfortable place, it's hard for you to change your habits. But being afraid to change something can hold you back from making life-changing decisions or improving yourself. Getting out of your regular rituals will boost your confidence and open up new doors in your life. Make a choice to break out of your routine and try something new.

Get Stepping

In terms of fitness, earth signs like measurable results. They like to be able to calculate situations and use concrete facts to do so. This is why a pedometer, smart watch, or fitness tracker would be perfect for you. You like to be able to know the exact number of steps you have taken so you can use that information to plan, to calculate further exercise or meals, or as a motivator for yourself. Those folks who go willy-nilly into exercise are not for you; hard facts and organization will get the job done for an earth sign.

Get Your Calcium

Capricorn rules over the bones and skeletal system; therefore, regular consumption of calcium is an important factor for you. Calcium is important because it strengthens bones, regulates blood pressure, aids in the secretion of hormones, and helps boost your metabolism. Without enough calcium, your body can be prone to osteoporosis, teeth problems, and pains in the knees, toes, and joints.

The easiest way to get more calcium is through dairy products like cheese, yogurt, and milk, but you can also find it in foods such as spinach and other leafy greens, nuts, grapes, oats, sardines, and calcium-fortified soy milk or tofu to name just a few. Or you can also try one of the many available calcium supplements too; just check with your doctor before choosing one.

Buy Some Black Tulips

The black tulip is a unique flower and one that appeals to Capricorn's love of the finer things in life. Once thought to be only a myth, the black tulip came into existence in the 1980s through the labor of a Dutch grower named Geert Hageman. Because black is one of Capricorn's signature colors, it fits perfectly to have a black flower. Like many things worth having, the black tulip may be harder to find, but it makes a special and unique gift. Treat yourself to a bouquet of black tulips and appreciate the beauty in something both individual and simple.

Buy Good Sneakers

As a Capricorn you need to take extra special care of your joints, especially the knees as yours are prone to injury. One way to take care of your knees is to make sure you buy good supportive sneakers for working out, particularly if you are a runner. Capricorn tends to only go for well-made, high-quality clothing pieces, so make sure you extend this habit to your workout footwear as well. Do your research (something Capricorn loves to do) and find the best brands and styles for your workout regimen. Don't forget to change your exercise shoes regularly, too, to always have the best support possible.

Do Some Heavy Lifting

—————

E arth signs are incredibly strong people, mentally and physically. With that in mind, make sure you emphasize weight and strength training in your workouts. Develop your lifting muscles by exercising with weights and concentrating on weight-bearing exercises throughout your life. There are so many variations of weight and strength training that you can easily find a routine that suits your age, strength, general health, and energy level. Strength training will help you fight the loss of muscle, bone mass, and strength that occurs naturally with aging. It is also great for your joints, an area of concern for a lot of earth signs.

Seek Out Terra-Cotta for
Your Outdoor Spaces

Terra-cotta is the perfect material for Capricorn to use in her garden, terrace, or other outdoor spaces. Terra-cotta is a kind of earthenware used since ancient times, and its name translates to "baked earth." Not only is it made from the earth (and Capricorn is an earth sign), but its dark red, burgundy, orange, and brown hues are all colors that Capricorn is drawn to. Add some terra-cotta pots to your terrace, put some terra-cotta statues in your garden, or hang a simple terra-cotta sculpture on an outdoor wall space. Feel the warmth of the color and the earth elements resonate with your Capricorn roots.

Heal Your Spirit with a Garden

You are an earth sign, after all. What could be more in tune with your nature than to work with the earth? As an earth sign, you tend to hold on to stress and have trouble releasing it, but working with the soil will bring you into a state of calmness. When you are connected to an element, just being near it and working with it can help realign your energy and bring peace.

So go out and till your soil, buy seeds or plants, and then plant them in precise and organized rows. As you watch your plants grow and tend to them, you will discover your stress will wash away. Even if you don't have space to plant a garden where you live, just getting your hands in the soil will help heal your spirit.

Give Yourself Some Time

E arth signs are grounded, logical, and reliable, so it goes without saying that you hate to be late. In fact, punctuality is an admired quality of the earth signs. If a situation occurs that causes you to be late, it can fill you with stress and cause anxiety. So, with that in mind, make a point of giving yourself some extra time to get where you need to be. This will give a cushion in case some unexpected events pop up and delay you. You know being late will stress you out, so do your mind and spirit a favor and try to eliminate anything that might interfere with your timeliness.

Meditate On
the Color Nut Brown

As a Capricorn you are driven and resilient, and always searching, but sometimes for your own mental happiness it is necessary to relax and just *be* for a few minutes. At least once a week (or more if your schedule allows), try to spend 10–15 minutes musing on one of your signature colors, nut brown. At first you may think brown is a boring color, but nothing could be further from the truth. Brown symbolizes warmth and the earth, and nuts symbolize the bounty of the earth. Brown is found in nature at all times of the year and represents stability and practicality. Brown is dependable and simple. Picture yourself in a forest in autumn surrounded by shades of warm brown and allow yourself to unwind and relax.

Keep Things Slow and Steady

Earth signs know that nothing great ever comes easily or quickly. In fact, their combined patience and discipline is one of their most admirable traits and allows them to stick things out for the long run. Earth signs like to meticulously plan and *hate* to rush. Actually, rushing through a task will cause you stress and may lead to mistakes (something you don't tolerate well). Whether working or playing, you should take a slow and steady approach, and your final results will be better quality and more long-lasting than those of the hurried competition. Keep a steady pace when at home and at work and you'll produce your best results.

Decorate with Pewter

Capricorn's home should be decorated in the style of the things she values, including permanence, reliability, structure, and tradition. She also has a love of fine things, and this will be obvious in the ornamentations she uses in her home. Because she rules over pewter, décor items for the Capricorn home should include some kind of pewter element as well. Pewter appeals to both Capricorn's love of history and her love of simple quality pieces in her home. Try a set of pewter candlesticks on your dark wood table or a few pewter accessories like picture frames or mirrors. If you know a fellow Cap, something pewter would also make an excellent gift for her home too.

Learn at Your Own Pace

As an earth sign, you love to learn new things and are not dissuaded when the subject seems difficult or arduous. Persistence is definitely an earth sign characteristic! But while you love to discover new skills, you don't like being monitored while you do so. You learn better while working solo and do not like to have someone looking over your shoulder. Often methodical and meticulous, you have no patience for those who want to just jump in and go with it. So don't put yourself through that! If you are part of a group for work or school, try suggesting that everyone work on ideas separately and then reconvene to discuss them. That way you can have your solo learning time while still being a team player!

Appreciate What You Have

Ambitious Capricorn is always reaching for the next challenge, the next mountain to climb, but it is important for your mental and spiritual health to take time to appreciate all that you have already accomplished and all that you already possess. Try to sit down daily and think of five to ten things that you are grateful for (extra points for thinking of even more!). Picture these things in your mind and let the feeling of gratitude and appreciation resonate in your body.

Sit quietly for 10 minutes or so each day and think of what you are grateful for and you will become a happier and more appreciative Capricorn!

Eat What You Love

E arth signs love their foods, and they especially like to be relaxed and savor their food when they eat it. However, many earth signs have sensitive palates and have to be choosey about what they eat. You need to listen to your body about what it needs and what it can tolerate, and when you find a food you like, enjoy it! Also, being conscious about what foods you are putting in your body is important for earth signs. When you can, try to choose foods grown without pesticides, added hormones, or artificial fertilizers as many of these things can irritate your body. Go with natural and organic versions of the foods you love.

Build Endurance with Your Workouts

E xercise is proven to be one of the best forms of self-care you can do for your body and mind. But what if you are new to working out or just feel like it isn't your thing? Fortunately for you as an earth sign, the slow and steady approach also relates to how you should be working out. Earth signs are disciplined, dependable, and committed. So, when they exercise, they should choose workouts that require patience, precision, and a set routine.

Workouts that work your muscles at a slower pace will build your endurance and muscle strength without making you feel like your regime is hectic and out of your control. Training for races that require precision and problem-solving like a Tough Mudder, which is more about endurance than speed, is also a hit with earth signs.

Find Some Black
Amethyst Glass

Capricorn loves history and especially antiques. Objects that harken back to a simpler traditional time give her a feeling of stability and comfort. Embrace that part of your sign by buying some black amethyst glass. Amethyst glass is a type of depression glass, glass given away by companies with purchases during the Great Depression as an incentive for consumers to do business with them. The glass would range in colors from the common pink, green, and amber to the rarer cobalt blue, purple, and black. This depression glass, now considered a valuable antique, is not only simple, sophisticated, and useful—all things you love—but its black to purple hue is one that Capricorn is also especially drawn to.

Find some black amethyst glass for your home; its form and function will match your Capricorn taste perfectly.

Indulge in the Warmth of Cinnamon

Nothing conjures up feelings of warmth like the smell of cinnamon. It brings back memories of warm, comforting foods on cool, crisp fall days. But cinnamon is not just for autumn time; in fact, it is perfect for earth signs to use all year round. When you're cooking, choose warm spices like cinnamon over sharp and peppery spices, as these tend not to agree with an earth sign's delicate palate. As an added bonus, cinnamon is good for your heart health, helps regulate your blood sugar, boosts your brain function, and offers your body protection from diabetes.

Cinnamon is a marvelous addition to both sweet and savory meals and will add the hint of spice you crave without the burning aftereffects of other spices. Add cinnamon to your favorite foods including oatmeal, pancakes, yogurt, peanut or almond butter, chilies and soups, and even your coffee!

Keep the Clutter Out

Capricorn's home décor is usually sleek and functional. Everything should be in its place. Still, even with this drive for form and function, occasionally your living spaces can get a bit untidy with the clutter of your busy life.

When this happens, it's important to set aside some time to clean out the clutter. Toss everything that doesn't improve your life and get back to the basic clean lines you gravitate toward. You'll be surprised what a boost it can be for your mental and spiritual health to get rid of the unwanted things that don't serve a purpose in your life.

Treat Yourself to Chocolate

E arth signs love chocolate, and it's a wonderful way to treat yourself. Some earth signs may have trouble with dairy though, so try a good-quality rich dark chocolate to indulge in. Not only does dark chocolate taste heavenly, but it benefits your health too. Dark chocolate helps lower blood pressure, is a powerful source of antioxidants, and reduces your heart disease risk. Eat your dark chocolate straight—or melt some in a double boiler, pour into a silicone mold ice cube tray, sprinkle on some healthy nuts and dried fruits, and allow to set for a mouthwatering treat you can feel good about.

Use a Blackboard

ometimes a little nostalgia is good for the soul. Capricorn loves tradition and history, so why not play on that theme a bit in your home (or even office) décor. Buy a small blackboard and some chalk, and put them in a central locale in your home. Use the board to write reminders, notes, doodles, and even jokes on. Revel in the feeling of nostalgia: the feel of the chalk in your hand, the sound of the chalk moving along the blackboard, the light smell of the dust. It will bring back memories. Embrace the old in a new and fashionable way with a blackboard in your living space.

Stick with the Classics

Treat yourself to a little shopping trip, but rather than buying the latest fad, shop for your sign. Style magazines and experts may tell you what's all the rage in fashion, but as an earth sign, you won't necessarily feel comfortable or strong—both things earth signs need in their lives—with what is trendy. Earth signs are all about the simple yet elegant look when it comes to fashion, as well as décor. You like things that are classic, well made, neat, and polished—think Audrey Hepburn (who is also an earth sign!) and George Clooney.

In terms of clothing, you feel more comfortable in the elegant and sophisticated and stay clear of the flashy, too tight, or too revealing. You value comfort, but that doesn't mean you don't look suave or glamorous; you like to make a statement without seeming like you are making a statement. So stick with the classics and you'll always exude an understated elegance.

Make a Family Tree

———————

Capricorn has a strong sense of family tradition and history. Why not expand on that trait and make a family tree! Discovering where you came from can give you great insight into who you are today. There are so many websites that can help you trace your ancestry, or you can ask relatives and loved ones to help you fill in the blanks. You can also find public records online that can give you clues about family members who have passed on or who lived long ago. Once you've collected all your data, you can compile it to create a beautiful piece of family history to display in your home.

Protect Your Throat

Earth signs are connected to several parts of the body including the throat. Communication is key to earth signs, and when something interferes with that communication, whether it be a blocked throat chakra or even a sore throat, earth signs' confidence and strength can suffer. So protect your throat! In the colder months wear a scarf or muffler around your throat. Try meditating with turquoise to open up your throat chakra. If you do get a sore throat, treat it quickly and naturally with a saltwater gargle, honey, lemon water, or ginger tea.

Calm Your Mind Before Bed

Capricorn is a work-centric person; you love to give things your all and are never one to back away from a challenge. But, as a result of all this strength of will and drive, you often find yourself burned out by the end of the day. After a long day of climbing those mountains, your body and mind need a break before falling asleep. It's important for Capricorn to take some time to quiet her mind before going off to bed.

Turn on a soft light or flameless candle, lie down or sit in a comfortable position, and close your eyes, exhale through your mouth and inhale through your nose three times, and think about nothing. That's right, nothing. Focus instead on relaxing every part of your body, from your head down to your toes. Visualize each part of your body letting go of its tension and releasing stress. Now turn off the light, and go enjoy a peaceful night's rest.

Reach for Your Goals

Once earth signs know what they want, they will stay the course until they get it. Earth signs are strong and disciplined people, so use that tenacity to achieve the things you want most in life. Use your detail-oriented, driven brain and create a goal board. List the things you most want to accomplish and post them up where you can see them every day. This way you can be sure to keep your goals fresh in your mind and on the top of your to-do list. Also make sure the goals you write on your board are clear and actionable. Whatever your goal is, this visual reminder is key to helping you stay focused and on track.

Create a Room of Comfort

Everyone needs a space, even if it is just one room in your house or apartment, where you can just get away and relax in comfort. Comfortable surroundings are important for earth signs in particular; not only do they crave them, but they also feel the most at peace there.

So make sure at least one room in your home is filled with plush, cushy furniture. Big pieces of furniture are important for comfort, too, because they give you a sense of security and a feeling that you are staying put. Overstuffed pillows and soft blankets would make nice accents here as well. Create a room that makes you feel safe and snug, a place you can go to find relaxation and peace and forget the stresses of your life, and you will be a truly happy earth sign.

Stretch First

Capricorn rules over the bones and joints and especially the knees. Capricorn also tends to have a lot of problems with these areas including cracking knees, joint pain, and arthritis. Consistent exercise can help with many of these problems, but it's important for your joints that you stretch first. Capricorn's drive can sometimes push her to work out too hard, so it's vital that you get your body limber to avoid any injury. Spend 8–10 minutes doing stretches before you start your workouts. Try some basic stretches like hip circles, walking lunges, calf raises, and hip flexor stretches to get your joints flexible and ready for your workout.

Wrap Yourself in Warmth

There is something so special and nurturing about being wrapped in something cuddly. Earth signs especially like to feel warm, protected, and comfortable. A good way to accomplish this feeling in your home is to find a thick, warm comforter for your bed. Bonus points if you can make one yourself, maybe even stitching in some pieces of a childhood blankie. Not a crafty person? There is no shortage of ultraplush comforters available to buy online. Try to get one in a deep, rich earth tone to compliment your earth sign! Want to kick the comfort up a notch? Try warming your sheets in the dryer right before you get into bed!

Indulge Your Inner Goat

The symbol for Capricorn is the Goat, so keep connected to your sign and indulge in some goat's milk and cheese. Goat's milk is high in calcium and helps build strong bones—and Capricorn is also strongly associated with bones and the skeleton. Goat's milk is also easier to digest than cow's milk, and since many a Capricorn suffers from some stomach issues, this is a plus. Goat's milk is a promising treatment for people with malabsorption issues like osteoporosis, a condition that Capricorn is often susceptible to. So try a little goat's milk for both your sign and your health.

Make Your Home Your Haven

Earth signs like to feel protected in their home, almost as if it were a sheltered cave. A feeling of enclosure may seem stifling to other signs, but for earth signs there is a comfort in the closeness and warmth. Emphasize that feeling in your home by decorating with darker colors and with accents such as lamps with shades to give off a soft glow in your rooms. This warm and welcoming shelter will make you feel protected and safe whenever you enter it.

Buy Some New Shoes

Nothing would honor your sign like indulging in a new pair of boots or shoes because Capricorn rules over the knees—and also the lower legs. Not only does Capricorn rule over these areas, but she must also take special care with them as Cap tends to suffer from knee and joint pain. So when you buy those new boots, make sure they are a high-quality product and made well. Cheap shoes will only lead you to foot and knee problems down the road, so splurge for a good pair. And being a sensible Cap, you won't go crazy buying a whole closet full of shoes, you'll go for a pair you can match with a variety of outfits and styles.

Color Your Home
Like the Earth

E arth signs tend to feel most at ease in their homes when they are surrounded by calming earth tones. Greens, browns, and whites are great choices to decorate your home. Of course, given your simple tastes, you'll want to make sure these colors are muted versions, nothing too garish or bright. Loud colors will actually take away from your comfort level at home, something you don't want to do. Also wood floors, dark finishes, and plain walls will all add to the elegance and polished feeling of your home while fitting in perfectly with your classic and understated vibe.

Go for the Sour

———————————

Capricorn, though she loves food and cooking, often does not do well with certain types of foods, especially the spicy ones. She does however have a taste for sour and fermented foods: vinegars, pickles, soy sauce, wine, even "sour" milk products like sour cream and certain cheeses, and more lemony tasting foods. Any food that gives you that little bit of pucker is a good fit for Capricorn. So indulge in a plate of sour pickles or put out a bowl of sour balls; your Capricorn taste buds will thank you.

Embrace Your Practicality

S ometimes earth signs get a bad reputation for their serious sides, but your practicality is really a positive thing. Earth signs are incredibly sensible and resourceful, and they have a talent for solving problems that others give up on. You come up with real-world solutions that actually work! You love to ponder and thoroughly understand a problem or concept, and like to make charts, graphs, or diagrams to further explore the topic. You stick with a problem through the long haul and come up with a solution that works—celebrate the positives of being the perfect problem-solver!

Try Some Teak Furniture

With her hardworking nature Capricorn has an appreciation for fine craftsmanship and respects when something is well made. With that in mind, when decorating your home and outdoor spaces, you could invest in some teak wood furniture. Teak is valued both for its durability and its water-resistance. The natural oil in teak gives it a greater natural water- and weather-resistance than many other types of wood, meaning your outdoor furniture will last longer, be protected from rot and many pests, and continue to look good for years to come. Longevity like that is important to Capricorn, so if you're looking for furniture that suits your tastes and also matches your sign, go for teak.

Take One Step at a Time

———————

Some people like to jump headfirst into a problem and work it out while trapped in the midst of it. Well that may be great for them, but the thought of it gives earth signs nervous feelings. Earth signs approach almost everything they do with a methodical, step-by-step approach. This method allows you to thoroughly understand exactly what you're getting yourself into, come up with a well-thought-out plan to solve it, and then actually resolve the issue. While it may take you a little more prep time than other people when faced with a problem, you often have a higher success rate too. Breaking down obstacles into clear steps makes earth signs the best problem-solvers around.

Commune with Birches

Birch trees are often associated with Capricorn, especially in Celtic druid astrology. The druids thought that "birch babies" were always stretching themselves thin in search of light. A birch baby is also highly driven, ambitious, and resilient, and a natural leader—all Capricorn traits! So embrace your birch heritage and plant one in your yard. Don't have a yard, or have a yard that can't accommodate a tree? Then go to a place where you can find birch trees (your local state park perhaps, or a nearby arboretum), and take some time to sit beneath them and feel the presence of these glorious trees.

Make Your Home
on the Ground Floor

E arth signs instinctually prefer to keep their feet planted firmly on the ground—so their homes should be, as well! Creating a safe, comfortable home is important to earth signs, since it gives them a place to focus on their creative impulses and build a space that's perfect for feeling stable and reenergized.

Ground floor apartments have plenty of perks, such as access to outdoor yard spaces and easier move-in days. And better yet, you'll recharge best in a home where you can easily see (and touch!) the ground. Skip the high-rise apartment, and go for something closer to the first floor instead.

Embrace Your Inner Elvis

Elvis Presley, "The King," was a Capricorn. Known as a consummate perfectionist who always set the bar high for himself (hello Capricorn!), Elvis dug all types of music from rock 'n' roll to country music. So embrace your fellow Capricorn and put on some Elvis tunes as you do your chores around the home, or any time you need a boost. Capricorn loves traditional rock 'n' roll, and there could be no better example than Elvis.

Become a Plant Parent

It should come as no surprise that earth signs find it reassuring to include touches of nature in their homes. Keep yourself centered and relaxed by surrounding yourself with plants. If you're not able to live in a place with easy access to the natural world, try bringing nature to you! City dwellers can plant window boxes or fill their apartments with different types of houseplants.

A window herb garden is a great place to start. Try common herbs like basil, chives, cilantro, oregano, or parsley, which can be great additions to any meal and have many other useful qualities. (Did you know basil is a natural mosquito repellent?) Go all-natural and see how many ways your new garden can benefit your daily life!

Stop the Hurried Pace

Capricorn feeds on challenge: when others quit, she pushes on. *Resilience, determination,* and *drive* are all words that describe the mighty Capricorn. Unfortunately, all that pushing and striving can take a toll on your mental health. It is especially important that Capricorn self-care involves some kind of mindful moments during the day. Being mindful simply means being aware of the present.

Stop for a moment and savor that steaming warm cup of coffee, take a moment to watch your kids playing, or pause and really listen to that song on the radio. Stop for at least 10 minutes out of your fast-paced day and enjoy your life right in the moment. A little mindfulness can lead you to a more peaceful life.

Save Your Seat

Earth signs are known for seeking stability in their lives—and their work environment is no different. No matter your organizational style or tasks at hand, a sturdy, well-designed office chair is a must-have for any busy earth sign. It isn't easy to get through the workday if you're uncomfortable and distracted. You'll be able to stay focused and work more productively if you're settled at your desk in a chair that's comfortable for you.

Not only will you be better able to concentrate at work, you'll also be taking care of your body. No more stiff necks or backaches for you!

Buy an Hourglass

Capricorn's ruling planet is Saturn and in mythology Saturn was the god of time. Saturn the planet was named so because not only was it the last planet able to be seen with the naked eye (in ancient times), but it has the longest observable orbit in the sky (around thirty years) and so was thought of as the keeper of time, or Father Time. Embrace your ruling planet's timely mythology and purchase an hourglass. The earliest of time-keeping devices, its connection to time-related symbolism is unmistakable. Hourglasses are also a symbol of balance and symmetry, things near and dear to the Capricorn heart, and to sit quietly and watch the rhythmic cascading of the sands through the hourglass is itself a form of relaxing meditation.

Buy an hourglass and add it to your home's décor as a reminder of your ruling planet. Or if an hourglass isn't your speed, you might prefer collecting antique clocks and watches as a good Capricorn hobby.

Send Flowers...to Yourself!

No matter the season, earth signs benefit from having plants around. Just like you need plants in your home, you also need some for your office. Especially during dreary rainy days or cold months, you'll need something to reframe your mind-set and spark a positive attitude throughout the day.

Try a monthly flower or plant subscription service to get your plant pick-me-up. Whatever your preference, treat yourself to the perfect desk accessory, with options ranging from handcrafted bouquets to potted plants...or even a succulent or two! No secret admirer is needed—these services will deliver plants of your choice to your desk all year round.

Find Strength with
Black Hematite

Hematite is a shiny dark stone with a strong metallic luster and is one of the best stones you can use to harness the energy of the earth for strength and to dispel negativity. It is a grounding stone that will help you feel more focused and less stressed. Capricorn tends to work herself to the point of exhaustion, and hematite can help bring you back to balance and ease the symptoms of stress and anxiety.

Hematite is an attractive stone and relatively inexpensive, so it can be often found in jewelry. Wearing a necklace or bracelet with hematite will keep the stone near your pulse points, maximizing its protective energy. Or if jewelry is not your thing, you can carry some hematite in your pocket. This strong protective stone will keep you emotionally and spiritually safe.

Choose Only the Softest Fabrics

Earth signs have a highly developed sense of touch, so choose soft materials for your clothes and sheets. Don't spend your day feeling distracted by an itchy wool sweater or spend all night tossing and turning on scratchy sheets. Restore your healthy skin (and cheerful attitude!) by choosing materials like cashmere, silk, organic cotton, and suede.

You'll prefer any materials or fabrics that touch your skin to be soft and comforting, so go ahead and splurge on high thread count sheets, fluffy towels, and warm, downy blankets.

Indulge in Comfort Food

Craving some mac and cheese? A homemade chocolate chip cookie? Maybe even a simple, classic PB&J (peanut butter and jelly)? Reliable earth signs sometimes need to reclaim their roots and find comfort in the well known and well loved.

After a long day indulge in your love of comfort food, whether that's a cheesy slice of pepperoni pizza or a gooey brownie still warm from the oven. Take an uplifting trip down memory lane with simple foods that remind you of your childhood. Enjoyed in moderation, these treats will keep your stomach full and your heart happy.

Play an Instrument

While Capricorn's practicality often makes others think that she is not creative or artsy, the truth is that Capricorn is typically an excellent musician. Capricorn is not deterred from the challenge of learning an instrument, nor is she afraid to put in the hard work necessary. In fact, Capricorn is quite efficient at playing instruments and can master them quickly. One of the best instruments for Capricorn is the bass guitar. It allows her to be the steady rhythm of a musical piece. Try your hand at learning an instrument. You might be surprised how playing it can give you both the structure you love and the fun you need.

Treat Your Sweet Tooth

E arth signs are known for their appreciation for the finer things and may enjoy opportunities to indulge. You might find you instinctually gravitate toward sweet flavors over anything savory. While it's certainly important to eat a balanced diet and enjoy everything in moderation, a sweet treat or two can be just the pick-me-up you need to improve a grumpy mood or curb an unhealthier craving.

Although you may prefer to stick with your reliable, tried-and-true favorites, prevent yourself from becoming "stuck" by looking for your sweet fix in unexpected places. Expand your cultural palate by trying food from different cuisines.

Climb a Mountain

No, not a metaphoric mountain, a real mountain. Just as it is for your symbol the Goat, mountain climbing is an ideal physical activity for Capricorn. Many people think mountain climbers are risk-takers, but in actuality mountain climbing takes a large amount of planning, training, and forethought, things that Capricorn is great at. Mountain climbing also relies on the Capricorn traits of determination and drive, and the ability to be present in the moment.

In addition to the mental benefits of this activity, there are also major physical benefits including stronger muscles and improved cardio strength. Try and find an instructor or course in your area, or try a course at one of the many indoor rock climbing facilities. Remember, if you can climb a mountain, you can do almost anything!

Find Balance for
Your Finances

_____

S elf-care isn't always about having fun—sometimes
it's simply about that sense of accomplishment
you get from checking off a task on your to-do list.
Perfect for practical earth signs, make sure to get
through those financial day-to-day activities, like
reviewing your budget or balancing your checkbook.

Earth signs can be cautious and like to have a
sense of security, instead of taking unnecessary risks.
A balanced earth sign is able to successfully manage
their cautious tendencies and their indulgences. That
careful decision-making can help you manage your
money well; earth signs have a natural awareness that
helps them judge their financial situation exactly. Just
make sure you're not obsessing over the task!

Find Your Way

Capricorn is known for her determination. Once she has carefully considered her options and decided which is the best path for her, Capricorn will not be daunted by any obstacle. Though her progress may be slow and steady, she will find her way.

A good way to reinforce this determination is to use a mantra. A mantra is a phrase that helps keep you focused on what your goals are and what matters to you. Mantras boost your self-love because they help you focus on all that you are capable of doing. As you are pursuing your goals, remember to repeat this Capricorn mantra: "I find a way." Because once you set your mind to it, there is no mountain you can't climb.

Sip a Martini

The famous superspy 007 was known for loving his martinis, and it turns out this is also the perfect cocktail for you, Capricorn. Based on the balance of its ingredients, martinis are well suited to your meticulous nature. Capricorn loves to be in control, and this classic and respectable drink often represents power and class. To make your classic dry martini, fill a cocktail shaker with 2½ ounces dry gin, ½ ounce dry vermouth, and ice. Shake (or stir) for about 20 seconds and then strain into a martini glass. Try your classic dry martini with a lemon peel garnish as this scent appeals to Capricorn's spirited earth nature.

Give Yourself a Time Limit

E arth signs are known for being hard workers; they're resourceful and know just how to tackle tasks to make them manageable. They're also notoriously persistent when they're working to achieve their goals. Being productive and getting things done feels great to driven earth signs.

Stay on top of your to-do list with this productivity hack! Simply set a time limit with a timer to get your task done. Since you know you only have a limited time frame, you'll stay focused, quicken your pace, and accomplish a lot more than you expected. You'll feel satisfied and proud of all you'll be able to complete.

Reward Your Patience

In today's fast-paced world, it's important to stay patient, even when lines are slow, orders are misplaced, and Mercury in retrograde causes all kinds of confusion with communication. Luckily, earth signs are known for their ability to stay calm and forgiving. That's a great quality to maintain, so make sure you reward yourself on those days when your patience has been truly tested.

Whether it's enjoying a glass of fine wine, listening to some new music, or splurging on something you've had your eye on for a while, make sure to protect yourself from negativity and do something relaxing and restorative for you and you alone.

Find Healing with Turquoise

Capricorn's birthstone turquoise is known for its healing properties. Turquoise also acts as a purification stone that can dispel negative energy and can be worn to protect you from outside influences. As a Capricorn you like (and sometimes need) to be in control of situations and when you aren't, you can become fierce. Meditation with turquoise can help you keep calm when things aren't going your way.

Either hold some turquoise in your hand, or—even better—wear a turquoise necklace as turquoise is associated with the throat chakra. Unlike standard meditation where you sit in silence, when you meditate with turquoise, you should chant a mantra such as "I am healed" out loud. You should also visualize a stream of energy from your heart to your throat to your crown and back again in a loop. Try this meditation for 10–15 minutes.

Dance It Off

You know it's important to take care of your body by exercising. But did you know that earth signs have a good sense of rhythm and may find a new workout routine through dancing? It's also a great way to add fun into an existing exercise schedule or try something new so your usual routine doesn't get boring.

Try a peaceful ballet class for discipline, or experiment with jazz and hip-hop for a fun, high-energy workout. Or look for other dance-inspired classes like Zumba or barre, which combine dance elements and workout styles for unique and challenging programs.

Indulge in Some Cashmere

Capricorn style is all about effortless sophistication. You love simple, perhaps understated, pieces, and though you may stay conservative and shy away from showing too much skin, you are always subtle and elegant. Classic pieces made with richer fabrics are key elements in your wardrobe and no fabric could be more luxurious than cashmere.

Cashmere wool comes from the soft undercoat of goats; its separation process from the coarser protective topcoat is time and labor intensive thus making it a more expensive fabric. But nothing can beat the silky feel and intense warmth of cashmere. If a cashmere sweater isn't in your budget, go for a scarf or socks. Anything in cashmere will fit into your sophisticated Capricorn taste.

Enjoy the Power of Music

E arth signs love music. When you're feeling stressed, try using music to relax yourself. If you find yourself in a difficult situation, try to take a break to re-center and calm down. Put on your headphones, and let the sound of the music soothe you and distract you from your worries. Experiment with different genres to see what works best for you.

You may even find it relaxing to do some singing yourself—even if it's only in the safety of your own shower!

Surround Yourself with the Scent of Pine

Capricorn's season is winter and so it's no coincidence that the scent of pine is a great choice for you to have in your home or work space. The aroma of pine is thought to encourage self-confidence, positivity, patience, and strength, all qualities Capricorn embodies. Pine also stimulates the circulation and helps with fatigue, so you can keep on task and going strong as goal-orientated Capricorn loves to be. Try using pine essential oils in a diffuser, burning pine-scented candles, or even bringing fresh greenery into your home as decorations.

Read Some Realism

Not only does reading improve your imagination, your memory, and your vocabulary, but it also is a known stress reliever. As a Capricorn you often take on too much and can work yourself to the point of exhaustion. When you need to take your mind off the stress of your work or personal life, try reading as an excellent way to relax and release tension. But what does Capricorn like to read?

Like in all areas of your life, as a Capricorn you tend to gravitate to the reality based. You are also a dedicated and persistent reader (huge volumes of works never intimidate you!). When you are not reading books related to your trade or profession (or books on successful people), you tend to lean toward books with characters who get to the bottom of things in practical ways. Books about struggles against poverty and other real-life obstacles are also preferred. Authors like J.D. Salinger, Zora Neale Hurston, Stephen Hawking, and Charles Dickens may top your list.

Train for a Marathon

Patient earth signs are in it for the long haul; their workout style is more marathon than sprint. These slow and steady athletes are disciplined and committed to achieving their goals.

Your body will thank you for taking on activities like running, biking, dancing, or even jump roping! You may even want to train to run a marathon, or participate in a triathlon, which will really test your endurance with a series of swimming, biking, and running challenges. These activities will keep you feeling refreshed and rejuvenated, while helping you develop strength and stamina.

Use Wintergreen
for Sore Muscles

While Capricorn is often associated with earthy smells like patchouli and cinnamon, she also likes brighter, lighter scents, too, like wintergreen and lime. Wintergreen is especially useful for Capricorn because it also doubles as an effective remedy for sore joints, particularly arthritis, and Capricorn is sometimes weak in those areas. Wintergreen is beneficial for joints because it stimulates blood circulation around affected tissues and muscles. To use wintergreen essential oil on your joints, dilute it according to instructions and massage as directed into your sore joints and muscles.

Go for the Goal!

If you're looking for a team sport, keep in mind the earth signs' tendencies to look for ways to use their strength and stamina. Try sports like soccer or volleyball that combine those skills. With team sports like these, you'll be able to take care of your body and develop strong, supportive friendships, all while having the added benefit of keeping your feet in your comfort zone...firmly on the ground.

Your endurance will keep you going from the beginning of the game to the very last second. And your goal-oriented nature is sure to keep you on the winning team as you help your team toward victory!

Spice Up Your Cooking

Capricorn loves to cook. The precise nature of a recipe and the balance of ingredients and flavors go naturally with her disciplined nature. You are also a traditional person and so you love homemade food, especially family recipes and comfort foods.

Next time you are cooking up a batch of winter stew (a classic Capricorn comfort food), try adding in some spices suited especially to your sign, rosemary and thyme. The earthy smells of these spices appeal to your earth sign nature. As an added bonus rosemary is known to boost alertness and focus, and thyme—in addition to having one of the highest antioxidant concentrations of any herb—helps reduce stress.

Get Thee to a Nunnery (Literally)

Capricorn loves history. She also feels a special affinity toward places connected with stone, land works, and buildings from the past. Aligning with this affinity for the historic and the traditional, Capricorn rules over old churches and cloisters. So go visit one! Choose a historical church or cloister made from earth and stone, nothing too modern or showy (remember Capricorn loves classic and simple). If your budget doesn't allow you to venture off to sites around Europe, then research the history and tradition of churches in your area.

Try a Stress-Free Workout

If the thought of running a marathon has you sweating already, don't worry! There are other workouts perfect for earth signs, like learning to work on a balance bar or taking some beginners' gymnastics skills classes. With your disciplined attitude, you'll be able to focus on improving your strength and stability while mastering these challenging skills.

These workouts can be a great way to take care of your body and keep it healthy and toned. But they can also be a much-needed opportunity to relax and compose yourself on an otherwise busy day. The focus you'll need to master carefully controlled movements will help take your mind off the stress of your day and give you a chance to recharge.

Get a Simple Tattoo

Capricorn is fiercely independent. So why not show your independence permanently by getting a tattoo (once you find a trained artist with a good reputation). Of course, being a Capricorn, the design you pick will be simple and elegant—no full back tattoos happening here. A small understated design in a simple color will showcase your individuality, your strength, and your uniqueness in a way that nothing else could.

You could ink the Capricorn zodiacal symbol or even the Capricorn constellation if you want to keep with your sign, or pick a personal design that carries a meaning for you. As suits your Capricorn taste, you'll most likely want the tattoo in a discreet place where only those you choose to let see will do so—not that you would care about the opinions of others anyway. After all, you are not getting this tattoo for them. You are getting it for you!

Buy the Best
(but Only Buy a Few)

When it comes to her wardrobe, Capricorn's closet may seem sparse by other sign's standards, but she is not concerned by it. Capricorn's wardrobe is comprised of practical, multifunctional pieces. She may not have as many pieces as other people do, but what she does have is well made, stylish, and elegant. Go with simple pieces that you can use in several different situations, and don't be afraid to stick to the basics; it is what makes you so down-to-earth and relatable. You'll be better off with a smaller amount of expensive but exquisite outfits than a multitude of cheaply made pieces.

Is your budget a little too tight to go for the high-priced stuff? Capricorn is not afraid to go hunting for designer finds at consignment or resale stores either. After all, it doesn't matter how you got it as long as you and it look good!

Heal Anxiety with Amber

Amber, though not usually associated with Capricorn, is a stone that can be beneficial for Capricorn's personality. Amber is said to promote relief of anxiety and stress, aid with mental exhaustion, and help eliminate worry. Purchase a piece of amber jewelry and wear it like a healing talisman to boost your positive energy and protect you from the bad. Amber is best worn directly against the skin so your body can absorb its healing properties, and it often feels warm as opposed to other stones or glass.

Stretch Your Workout Routine

Earth signs enjoy having an established routine they can count on, so try developing a well-rounded workout routine that works for you. Add stretching as a consistent part of your routine to keep you feeling strong and healthy. Stretching can also prevent more serious injuries throughout your workout. Since stretching keeps your muscles flexible and relaxed, it's a perfect release if you're feeling stiff from a long day in the office, or even just tense and stressed. This easy, revitalizing addition to your workouts will make your body feel great.

Use Yoga to Recharge

Working out is all about finding the right balance. Try mixing your weights and cardio with yoga stretches to keep muscles limber. Think yoga isn't right for you? Don't worry—there are many different styles and class types, so you'll be able to find the perfect, restorative approach that's right for you and your body's needs.

By adding yoga into your routine, you may find yourself becoming stronger and more flexible. But your brain will also benefit by getting a break from thinking, worrying, and stressing. Since it's important to focus your awareness on your body and concentrate on performing each pose as best you can, you'll find your worries can take a back seat while you recharge.

Find Your Inner Ballet Dancer

———————

Capricorn's self-control and discipline are unmatched by any other sign, so it makes perfect sense that she is well suited to the rigors of ballet dancing. Ballet dancing takes both great ambition and a work ethic to succeed, two things Capricorn is known for. Capricorn's methodical goal setting and unrelenting attitude when faced with a challenge make her able to put in the hard work necessary to succeed in ballet dancing. Sign up for a class yourself and experience the challenge and the beauty of ballet.

Look Before You Leap

Earth signs are logical thinkers, who often like to fully evaluate their options before making a decision. They're seeking safety and security, so they aren't interested in taking big risks. Taking that essential time to think things through can be a major benefit for their mental health. You certainly don't want to be rushed into making a decision!

If you find yourself faced with a problem or challenging situation, think it over privately before confiding in a friend. Give yourself permission to reclaim the time and space you need for yourself. You'll feel more confident sharing your decisions and more comfortable moving forward.

Get Your Hands Dirty
with Pottery

Being an earth sign, Capricorn naturally loves things associated with the earth and physical realm, and she's not afraid to get a little dirty. Find and join a local class on pottery making, one where you can use a potter's wheel and get your hands in some clay. Many ceramics studios offer these classes, or, once properly trained, if you are feeling particularly ambitious, you can buy your own potter's wheel and create at home. The feeling of the clay and water stimulates Capricorn's artistic side and brings her closer to the earth.

Meditate in Nature

———————————

It's important to take a few moments to yourself to relax, refresh, and gather your thoughts. To get some peace of mind, try meditating in nature. Particularly for thoughtful earth signs, this time-out ritual can be helpful to clear your mind.

One option is to find a comfortable seated position, close your eyes, and focus on your breathing and the present moment before allowing yourself to pay attention to the natural world around you. Or try meditating while walking and see how nature interacts with each of your senses. What sounds can you hear? What are you able to touch? How does your body feel? Earth signs may find it particularly helpful to meditate on the flowers and trees around them.

Reduce Stress with Grounding

I t's no surprise that earth signs should be in close contact with the earth itself. One way to literally connect with the earth is to try "grounding," or standing or walking barefoot outside on the grass, soil, or sand. Not only does being barefoot outside just feel good, it may also reduce stress and inflammation while improving your circulation and mood. Try to spend 30 minutes a day grounding—either all at once or broken up into smaller chunks of time. Afterward, you'll find yourself relaxed, restored, and recharged.

Get a Deep-Tissue Massage

Capricorn's ligaments and joints take daily wear and tear, and problems with them can become an issue for her. To combat this, try a deep-tissue massage to help your body relax. Deep-tissue massage impacts deep layers of muscle and connecting tissues known as fascia, and has been used to treat pain and musculoskeletal ailments, and strain in joints and tendons, for thousands of years. Deep-tissue massage can lead to improvements in pain, stiffness, range of motion, and the overall function of your joints. Contact a local massage therapist and schedule a deep-tissue massage for your joint health!

Add a Soundtrack to Your Daily Chores

Sometimes, chores get to be boring and stressful for even the most practical and grounded of earth signs. And whether it's breaking out the vacuum cleaner or dusting every horizontal surface in your home, everyone has that one task that seems so unpleasant and difficult to finish.

For earth signs this is the perfect time to turn to your love of music to keep yourself mentally alert and refocus yourself on the task at hand. Whistling while completing your everyday tasks will keep you relaxed and help you tackle even your least favorite chores with ease.

Go Forest Bathing

Just like regular bathing involves immersing yourself in water, forest bathing is the process of immersing yourself in trees and nature. The Environmental Protection Agency recently found that the average American spends 93 percent of their time indoors, but earth signs especially benefit from regular contact with Mother Earth.

Forest bathing is an easy, relaxing way to enjoy the outdoors. Silence your devices so you savor your senses—see the various shades of green, smell the various flowers, feel the crisp air, and listen to the crunch of branches under your feet.

Learn to Delegate

If there is one thing Capricorn dislikes doing, it's handing off a part of her workload. To Capricorn there is only one right way to do something, and her way is the right way. But rather than work long hours poring over a complicated and difficult project, it is critical to your self-care to learn to delegate. Capricorn is prone to letting her work life overshadow her home and personal lives—all of which is not good for mental well-being! Next time you are assigned a project, take it and break it down into smaller parts. Then find some of those smaller parts to delegate out to your coworkers. Perhaps one of them is very apt in an area that isn't your forte.

This self-care task may be difficult for you, but it is essential to reducing your stress levels at work.

Declutter Your Home
and Your Mind

E arth signs are known to hang onto too many belongings. While you may enjoy the memories that these items bring, keeping too many of them will eventually clutter your physical and mental space.

Take a day to go through your possessions and decide what's most meaningful to you. If an item has outlasted its usefulness to you, donate it to someone who would enjoy it more. When you've finished, take notice of the physical space you've created and meditate in or near it for a few minutes if possible. You'll likely find that you've also freed up mental space for new ideas.

Smile!

Capricorn can have a reputation for being too serious and sometimes rigid. The simple solution is to smile frequently. Facial expressions have been shown to influence how you feel. So, if you are looking for a way to instantly give yourself a boost of happiness, try smiling more. It's simple. Think of someone you love and it will bring a natural smile to your mouth and sparkle to your eyes. Try smiling more throughout your day; hold the smile for 1 minute and you will feel your day getting better and happier!

Detox with a Mud Mask

After a long day, nothing feels better than a relaxing facial mask. And what better type for an earth sign than a mud mask? Clear away the pollutants and bacteria your face is exposed to on a daily basis using an element of the earth itself.

If time and your budget allow, you can visit a spa for a mud mask—but if that's not possible, pick one up at a drugstore or natural foods store and apply it yourself at home, taking slow, deep breaths as you let the mixture sit on your face. You'll find this detox to be especially restorative and cleansing.

Boost Your Business Look

Capricorn is a big career person. She is a hard worker who loves to lead and succeed. She can often be (although not always) found in the business world, but no matter where she works, she is usually the driven, determined, and dedicated leader. When it comes to fashion and style, she gravitates toward simple, sophisticated, and often business-like attire, so why not further embrace that idea and buy yourself the ultimate in business chic: a briefcase.

Not only does a briefcase suit your uber-organized mind-set, but its style and function fit perfectly with your no-nonsense personality. Try a briefcase in your signature colors like brown, black, or burgundy.

Paint a Rock

E arth signs like to be crafty, so let your creativity shine by painting a symbol of the earth—a rock! Head outdoors to find a few suitable rocks—usually, flat, smooth ones are the easiest canvas. You might want to start by painting a base layer of white paint so other colors show up better. Add details or hand lettering with fine-tip permanent markers.

Let the experience be quiet and meditative—listen to ambient music as you paint. When your design is complete, cover it with a clear coat of Mod Podge (following the directions) to seal it in. You can keep the rock for yourself as a reminder of your connection to the earth, or pass along its good energy and give it as a gift to a friend or loved one.

Try an Exotic Flavor

Capricorn is a traditionalist and that normally goes for her food preferences as well. You tend to like traditional foods, and will balk if someone tries to change them on you—may the stars help anyone who tries to serve you anything but turkey on Thanksgiving! But, just this once, break out of your food comfort zone and try something different or exotic.

Korean kimchi would be a good bet for Capricorn as it is filled with vegetables and on the salty side—a flavor that Capricorn usually gravitates toward. Kimchi can be found at almost any supermarket, or find a good recipe and follow the directions carefully to make your own at home. (A challenge any Capricorn would be up for!)

Set a New Goal for Yourself

M any people use the start of a new year to set goals. But there's no need to wait for January 1 to do that. As an earth sign, you'll benefit from setting a practical goal for yourself, and then tracking your progress, no matter what time of year it is. Whether you're trying to get rid of a bad habit or institute a healthy new one, setting a goal and noting checkpoints along the way makes you much more likely to be successful.

When you think of a goal, write it down and post it in a place where you'll see it frequently. Be sure to reward yourself every time you meet one of your checkpoints to keep yourself motivated.

Visit an Ancient Tree

Capricorn tends to love history, whether that be in the form of learning about historical time periods, collecting antiques, or researching family ties. She has a love of all that is old and historic. Explore that love of history in a new way by visiting ancient trees throughout your area. Trees and the earth are tightly tied to Capricorn, and the history associated with a long-standing tree will add to her enjoyment. Or take an ancient tree vacation. For example, the Woodland Trust (www.woodlandtrust.org.uk) keeps an ancient tree inventory of the oldest and most important trees in the UK. Plan a trip around visiting some of them and revel in the history!

Treat Yourself to
New Loungewear

E veryone owns some favorite sweats or comfy shirts. But many of us wear this loungewear until it's ripped, stretched out, and stained. Take stock of what you currently own and see if some of it can be recycled or donated. Then treat yourself to some new items, and enjoy them the next time you're unwinding at home after a long day in less-than-comfortable work clothes.

Earth signs love to be comfortable, so repeat this process once a year. You'll look forward to relaxing and recharging in your new pieces!

Add Some Zing with Vinegar

Capricorn loves to cook and her dedication and patience makes her an excellent chef. But, being a traditionalist, she often doesn't stray from her standard recipes or flavors. Next time you are in your kitchen whipping up a meal for your family or friends, try adding some vinegars to your dishes to bring them up to the next level. Adding an acidic component like vinegar to savory foods can up the flavor and do wonders for your dish. Drizzle some balsamic vinegar on your pizzas or flatbreads, add strawberry vinaigrette to fruit salad, or make some blueberry-balsamic barbecue sauce—the options go on and on.

Try Aromatherapy

E arth signs are closely in touch with all of their senses. Aromatherapy is a simple and easy way for you to connect with and savor your sense of smell. You can enjoy a citrus body wash to energize yourself during your morning shower, sip some ginger tea to recharge in a midafternoon slump, read in a room scented by a soothing vanilla candle, or spritz (diluted according to instructions) lavender essential oil on your pillow before bed to relax.

When you begin practicing aromatherapy regularly, you'll find yourself more in tune with your sense of smell all the time. You'll notice the scent of your neighbor's flowers, the mixture of flavors wafting from your favorite restaurant, and the earthy smells after a spring rain.

Volunteer for an Environmental Cause

Donating your time and effort to a cause you're passionate about is a great way to show you care about the world around you—and yourself. After all, research shows that people who volunteer are less stressed, have more friends, and are more confident! As an earth sign, honor your connection to the planet by volunteering for a group that protects the environment, reduces pollution, encourages people to get outside, or safeguards animals.

There are many ways to help, including performing manual labor, organizing fundraising, and offering skills like bookkeeping or web design. You will feel fulfilled and proud—and your work will be making a difference.

Cuddle with a Panda

C uddle with a panda stuffed animal, that is! Despite appearances, a panda actually has a lot in common with Capricorn. In addition to the simple and basic color scheme of a panda (something any classic Capricorn can appreciate), as a spirit symbol pandas are also associated (like Capricorn) with tenacity in the pursuit of a goal. The panda also represents privacy and personal boundaries, things that Capricorn also values. Bring the spirit of the panda into your home by keeping a panda stuffed animal in your bedroom. The comfort and peacefulness it brings will resonate throughout your room and make it a perfect place to relax and retire.

Decorate with Granite

Capricorn is the ruling sign of minerals and rocks; you are an earth sign, after all. So, when decorating your home, especially your kitchen and bathroom spaces, you should choose materials made from stone for your countertops. Both granite or marble would make excellent choices and stay in line with your Capricorn desire for well-made but versatile items. You could also try soapstone countertops as well.

Get Outside!

———————

L ying on the couch after work might have become routine for you, but what if you switched your habit? Earth signs are prone to becoming lethargic, so try to get outside for a walk almost every evening after you eat.

Walking will aid digestion, help you stay fit, and encourage you to decompress and unwind in a healthy way. Vary your route periodically to keep the walk from getting boring. An evening stroll is also a great way to engage with your community—say hi to people you walk by, buy lemonade from a kids' stand, or even join in a pickup basketball game.

Visit a Farmers' Market

Farmers' markets offer an astounding array of local produce and homemade foods. You might be surprised at what's being grown right around you. There's sure to be a market in your area—find out its schedule and pop in regularly. Let your senses savor the offerings—see the brightly colored displays, smell the fresh peaches and herbs, and maybe snag a sample bite that a stall is offering. Look for organic produce, which is good for the environment and your health.

Try to find recipes that use your farmers' market haul for a couple of dinners a week, and grab the whole fruits for easy snacks on the go.

Recharge Yourself
with Quartz

O nce thought by the ancients to be a kind of magical ice sent by the gods, quartz crystals are a natural healing stone. They are thought to stimulate the immune and circulatory systems and bring balance to the body. They also help with memory, concentration, and the filtering out of distractions. With Capricorn's concern for intellect, self-discipline, and balance, this is a perfect stone for you to use in your home. Put a clear crystal cluster by your window and let it soak up the sun. It will provide your living space with the positive vibrations you need to recharge your energy and find balance.

Ease Your Body
with Tea Tree Oil

I n addition to many other body parts, Capricorn is
also the ruling sign over the skin, so skin problems
are often issues for you. Luckily, tea tree oil (diluted
according to instructions) may help certain skin conditions; ask your doctor for guidance.

Tea tree oil is a common and readily available
essential oil, and Capricorn is often drawn to its spicy
earthy scent. It is also claimed diluted tea tree oil is
good for arthritis pain in joints, another area of concern for Cap, as it is able to penetrate and desensi-
tize irritated nerve endings.

Live It Up on Weekdays!

There's no need to wait for a weekend to go out for dinner or a night on the town! As an earth sign, you probably enjoy structure and routine, but you don't want to fall into ruts either. To avoid that, shake things up and enjoy a concert on a Monday evening, head out to dinner at a new restaurant on a Tuesday night, or go dancing on Wednesday after work. You'll release any stress you've been holding onto and take the pressure off your weekends to supply *every* bit of fun in your life.

Keep a Tuxedo

This may seem like strange advice, but for Capricorn it fits perfectly. Capricorn takes everything in her life seriously and that includes fashion. Capricorn sticks to classics in and out of the workplace, and traditional business attire is the cornerstone of her wardrobe. Capricorn, regardless of gender, also tends to lean toward traditional menswear elements, like formal pants, suit jackets, and military-inspired styles (for women, think Diane Keaton or Marlene Dietrich). With that said, one on the best ways to exemplify your classic style and taste is to wear a tuxedo (tailored perfectly, of course) to your next posh event. The structured lines and impeccable look of a well-made tuxedo will make any Capricorn feel like a star.

Invest Your Money

Earth signs are conscientious—money matters tend to come easy for you. Still, you want to be sure that your money isn't just sitting in an account somewhere. Put it to work for you by making wise investments.

Do some research with trusted sources to be sure your investments are smart, and work with a broker or on your own to make the actual transactions. Check in periodically to see how your accounts are doing and make adjustments as needed. Over time, your investments will grow and you'll enjoy even more fortune.

Try an Empowering Mantra

With Saturn as her ruling planet, Capricorn is often self-disciplined and hardworking. She is highly organized, highly efficient, and highly dedicated to becoming a success. With those traits in mind, here is a mantra you can repeat to yourself or out loud to reinforce your inner power. Simply sit in a quiet place and clear your mind. Take a few deep breaths and start saying the mantra "I build the structure of my life" out loud several times. Then take a few minutes to think about what that mantra means in your life. If you find your mind wandering, simply refocus it. Try this meditation for 15 minutes each day and feel your self-confidence grow.

Wear More Leather

———

Capricorn likes her clothes to be of high quality and versatile in many different situations—multitasking outfits that are just as multitalented as her! She likes clothing that is practical and has a purpose, but she cannot bear shoddy workmanship. As a result, Capricorn does well in fabrics like leather that can be at home in a chic restaurant or a trendy cocktail bar.

Leather is also ideal for Cap because it is most often seen in earth tones, especially brown and black, which are perfect for simple yet sophisticated Capricorn. Whether it be gloves, belts, jackets, or coats, you should try incorporating more leather into your wardrobe both for ease and appropriateness, but also for elegance and glamour.

Spring for an Expensive Bottle of Wine

L ife is too short to ~~drink inexpensive~~ wine *all* the time. Every once in a while, treat yourself to an expensive, high-quality bottle of wine. As an earth sign, you can appreciate the finer things in life, and you have a great sense of taste. Ask an employee at your local liquor store for a recommendation based on your preferences, or reach for a longtime favorite of yours.

Take out your nice glassware, let the bottle breathe, and then swirl and sip slowly so you can really taste the subtle notes in the glass as you relax and unwind.

Try to Compromise

E arth signs have so many wonderful qualities, but one characteristic that might trouble you some-times is your stubbornness. Instead of getting down on yourself, turn that trait around by consciously working to compromise whenever possible.

For example, if a friend wants to go out to one type of restaurant and you want another, talk for a few minutes to determine someplace you'd both like. If your partner prefers one couch but you want to buy another, work out a solution based on what's best for your space. These types of thoughtful, caring conver-sations go a long way toward ensuring harmony in your relationships.

Get Back to Nature

As a Capricorn you need to have everything under control; however, life doesn't always go that way, and this can lead to you feeling stressed and frustrated. Capricorn needs to remember that sometimes you just have to go with the flow of life and relax, and a perfect way to do that is to go for a nature hike. Capricorn does great with steady exercise that you can do at your own pace and hiking certainly fits that bill. Also, the act of physically getting away from your stress and work is key for Capricorn to find some relaxation and relief. So get out in nature and take a hike! You and your stress level will both benefit.

Create Your Own Pottery

You've probably seen gorgeous pottery in stores, but have you ever tried to make it yourself? For a fun activity, work with some clay to make your own creation, be it a simple bowl, a mug for your morning coffee, or a decoration to give as a gift. Earth signs are in touch with their senses, and this hands-on craft allows you to get your hands dirty and really savor your sense of touch.

Take a class at a local art center or craft store where you can make a piece from start to finish. Once you've made your creation, you can have it fired by the professionals in its natural color or painted.

Daydream to Calm Your Mind

In today's world it's easy to have your brain running nonstop. Work, family, and other responsibilities are on your mind—you probably jump from one practical thought to the next with no break. It's time to change that and give your head a break!

Allow yourself time to daydream about something positive every day—whether it's while you shower in the morning, during your lunch break, or before you go to bed. Banish thoughts of bills or deadlines and think of something wonderful—a favorite vacation spot, a warm memory with a loved one, or a life goal you're trying to achieve. You'll find this practice leaves you mentally energized, refreshed, and balanced.

Incorporate Your Life Into Your Décor

———————————

Capricorn loves her job or main hobby and is often very passionate about it. So use that passion in your décor as well! Try and find pictures or paintings of people doing what you do, or things related to it. Or, if that's not possible, try framing your achievements and your family's achievements, things like degrees, photographs of winning awards, or noteworthy actions. Of course you'll want to make sure all your frames match and fit into your classic and refined taste. Coming home and seeing these things will make you feel more at ease and put a smile on your face.

Go the Distance

When it comes to exercise, Capricorn prefers things that require a long steady haul rather than quick bursts of energy—you are definitely not made for the HIIT (high intensity interval training) workouts. Triathlons, cross-country skiing, hiking, and even marksmanship would all be activities that would appeal to you. When other signs give up, Capricorn will persevere on. You are not afraid to take up a time-intensive challenge and see it through to the end. If you find your exercise routine is lacking, then seek training in an activity that requires endurance over speed.

Whip Up a Delicious
Green Smoothie

Feeling tired, hungry, and de-energized during a late afternoon slump? Instead of overindulging in an unhealthy snack you eat mindlessly, restore yourself with a smoothie made with fresh, leafy greens from the earth. Kale, arugula, and spinach are good sources of folate, fiber, and vitamins A and C, plus they are filled with antioxidants and are known to improve heart health.

Grab one at a juice bar near you, or make your own, adding chunks of pear, honey, or apple to the greens to create a bit of sweetness in your drink. Savor each sip, and notice how it makes you feel restored and rejuvenated with no guilt!

Incorporate Your Colors
Into Your Life

Being a winter sign, Capricorn's colors lean more toward the earthy tones. Black, burgundy, hunter green, navy blue, and brown are all colors that suit Capricorn. Try to incorporate these colors into your home décor and wardrobe. Brown or black leather (real or faux) furniture would be ideal for your home; also natural woods would look great. For clothing go with a classic little black dress, or stylish navy blazer. Winter white would also fit your Capricorn nature perfectly.

Indulge in a Day Off

Earth signs are very practical and dependable, but they can take that dedication too far and end up overworking themselves. Treat yourself to days off from work or life periodically to recharge your batteries. A mental health day can do wonders for your happiness, creativity, and health.

Be sure to take the whole day to relax—don't fill it up with errands and appointments. Go for a long walk outside, enjoy a coffee at a local café, take a warm bath... Spend your time focusing on what your body needs to restore itself—you deserve it!

Try a New Spin on an Old Favorite

***

Capricorn enjoys salty flavors, and that can lead to you overdoing it on the salt in your recipes. Try a new twist on salt with sour salt. Sour salt is actually citric acid and adds a nice pucker to certain recipes during cooking (it should not be used as a table salt substitute however). Sour salt is sometimes used as an addition to lemonade and is perfect for making sourdough bread (which appeals to Capricorn's earthiness). Make sure to research appropriate recipes and follow the sour salt directions for correct use of this interesting ingredient. So jazz up your taste buds and give sour salt a try.

Breathe Away Worry

Worry is a Capricorn trait. You are always striving for more and worrying about what mountain you will need to climb next. But all that worry is not healthy for your mental well-being, so breathe it away! Try this simple breathing exercise to release some worry from your life.

Sit down in a comfortable chair or on the floor. Sit with a straight back and rest your hands on your lap. Close your eyes and just sit for a moment, getting accustomed to how you feel. Now it's time to get breathing. Take a deep breath in through your mouth or your nose, fill your lungs completely and hold the breath for one second, and then exhale deeply, emptying out your lungs. Pay attention to the slow, steady rise and fall as you breathe. Continue breathing with this method for 3 minutes, or at least twenty breaths. Notice how much calmer and more collected you feel afterward!

Talk to a Friend

These days we often rely on texting to keep in touch with friends. While that's a good method a lot of the time, it's also vital to keep friendships strong by talking on the phone or, even better, in person. Earth signs are very loyal, and your friends are important to you. Show them that by prioritizing them in your schedule. Find time to catch up so you can move past emojis and nurture the type of close bond you and your friend deserve.

If finding a mutually agreeable time is proving difficult, get creative—for example, take a walk or jog together so you can exercise *and* catch up.

Discover Calm with Patchouli

Patchouli has a deep, earthy smell that resonates well with Capricorn. And while the scent often has a bad rep, being associated with tie-dye and head shops, it is actually an ancient herb from the mint family. The musky earthiness of patchouli can help both slow your mind and stimulate your nervous system, uplifting your mood. As a Capricorn you work tirelessly (almost stubbornly) toward your goal and push yourself sometimes beyond your limits. Patchouli can work wonders on healing the emotional and psychological impact of this stress, and can help with feelings of anxiety and burnout. Use patchouli essential oil (diluted according to instructions) on a warm compress applied to your forehead and try a little mellow relaxation.

Listen to Some Oldies

L istening to some classic tunes may not seem like an obvious way to care for yourself, but the impact of music on mood is actually well documented. When you listen to upbeat music, your mood improves. Classic or traditional music is important for Capricorn because she is disciplined and family orientated. She, therefore, tends to prefer the type of music her parents raised her on. So, whether it's classical or classic rock 'n' roll, listen to some oldies but goodies for an uplifting mood enhancer!

About the Author

Constance Stellas is an astrologer of Greek heritage with more than twenty-five years of experience. She primarily practices in New York City and counsels a variety of clients, including business CEOs, artists, and scholars. She has been interviewed by *The New York Times*, *Marie Claire*, and *Working Woman*, and has appeared on several New York TV morning shows, featuring regularly on Sirius XM and other national radio programs as well. Constance is the astrologer for *HuffPost* and a regular contributor to Thrive Global. She is also the author of several titles, including *The Astrology Gift Guide*, *Advanced Astrology for Life*, *The Everything® Sex Signs Book*, and the graphic novel series Tree of Keys, as well as coauthor of *The Hidden Power of Everyday Things*. Learn more about Constance at her website, ConstanceStellas.com, or on *Twitter* (@Stellastarguide).

Stand As Strong As a Mountain

Mountain Pose is an ideal yoga pose for Capricorn. Capricorn is as sturdy and strong as the mountains, and this pose helps personify that lofty image. Capricorn also rules over the joints in the body, and this pose works on strengthening those areas.

To do Mountain Pose, simply stand tall and proud with your feet together. Soften your kneecaps so you don't lock or hyperextend your knees. Next, imagine a line of energy all the way from your legs, up your spine, and out through the crown of your head. Your entire body should be straight on this center line; tuck your tailbone and bring your pelvis into a neutral position. Press your shoulder blades back, but don't squeeze them together. Keep your arms straight, fingers extended, and triceps firm. Breathe slowly and feel your spine elongating. Keep your eyes on the horizon and visualize the strong impenetrable mountain that you are.